STOCK MARKET INVESTING

A Guide for Beginners with Strategies &
Technical Analysis to Understand
How to Become a Profitable Investor
Creating Cash Flow Thanks to Options & Forex
(Part 1)

By **James N. Miles**

Table of Contents

CHAPTER 1:

ABOUT THE STOCK MARKET

DEFINITION AND BACKGROUND

A stock is a kind of security that connotes proprietorship in a partnership.

It speaks to a claim on the part of the partnership's advantages and income. It is additionally alluded to as "offers" or "equity." It is utilized to symbolize a financial specialist's possession in an organization.

The individuals who claim stock are usually called stockholders or investors. As an investor, a speculator theoretically argues a level of everything the organization possesses or owes. The organization's productivity or scarcity in that department decides if its stock is traded at a sequential cost.

It is given by organizations to raise capital to develop the business or attempt new undertakings. The stock (likewise capital stock) of an enterprise is established of the equity stock of its proprietors.

A single portion of the stock speaks to fragmentary responsibility for the company concerning the complete number of offers. The capital of a partnership is parceled into shares, the aggregate of which is expressed at the hour of business development.

The current investors might approve new offers given by the organization. In certain locales, each portion of stock has a specific pronounced standard worth, which is a notable bookkeeping term used to speak to the equity on the financial record of the company. In other words, however, portions of stock might be given without related standard worth.

Classes of Shares

A business may offer various sorts (or classes) of offers, each having particular possession rules, benefits, or offer qualities. The issuance of a stock declaration records responsibility for might.

1. A **stock endorsement** is an authoritative report that determines the measure of offers claimed by the investor, and other points of interest of the offers, for

example, the standard worth, assuming any, or the class of offers.

Typically, the stock appears like portions of either common stock or favored stock. The qualification between the two will be examined:

2. **Common Stock**, for the most part, qualifies the proprietor for a vote at investor's gatherings and to get profits. These are the stocks when people utilize the term with regards to a portfolio.

In current occasions, the common stock is virtually given as "completely paid" and "non-assessable", which implies once you have procured it, you can't be compelled to pay any more cash.

That is, your potential misfortunes are limited to what you have contributed.

3. **Favored Stock**, by and large, doesn't have to cast a ballot right; however, it has a higher claim on resources and income than the common stock. It is legitimately qualified for getting a specific degree of profit installments before any profits can be given to other investors.

For instance, owners of favored stock get profits before typical investors and if an organization fails.

Besides those two classes of stock, which are typical and both now and then are utilized in putting resources into the stock market as the significant classes of shares of stock.

There are still a few classifications of shares of stock that one should know to have a foundation.

In this manner, other characterizations of portions of stock are exhibited and separated dependent on their possession rights, organization points of interest, and on their relative size.

4. Various Types of Stocks and Stock Classifications

Because of Ownership Rights

This is the most fundamental parameter for characterizing stocks. For this situation, the giving organization chooses whether it will sell regular, liked or mixture stocks. There are two unique sorts of stock that financial specialists can possess. They have diverse possession rights and various benefits.

a. Common Stock

The underlying stock is as it sounds, normal. At the point when people converse about stocks, they are typically alluding to the underlying stock, and the incredible lion's share of stock is given in this structure.

Regular stock speaks to proprietorship in an organization and a claim on a segment of that organisation's benefits (profits). Financial specialists can likewise cast a ballot to choose the Board of Directors who administer the choices made by the executives.

Indeed, the underlying stock has given more significant yields than practically all other regular venture classes. Notwithstanding the most significant returns, the underlying stock likely additionally conveys the most noteworthy risk.

If an organization fails, the primary investors won't get cash until the lenders, bondholders and favored investors are paid. This risk can be extraordinarily diminished by owning a wide range of entrenched organizations (expansion) that have strong fiscal summaries and a past filled with a solid income.

b. **Favored Stock**

Favored stock speaks somewhat of proprietorship.

The organization, however, for the most part, doesn't accompany similar democratic rights. With favored offers, financial specialists have generally ensured a fixed profit. This is not quite the same as underlying stock, which has variable profit installments that vacillate with organization benefits.

In contrast to regular stock, the favored stock doesn't, for the most part, appreciate (or deteriorate in market downturns) in stock value, which brings about lower general returns.

One bit of leeway of a favored stock is that in case of insolvency, favored investors are paid off before the regular investor (yet after obligation holders). I like to consider the favored stock as being some place in the middle of bonds and regular stock. It imparts likenesses to both.

As an outcome, I wouldn't hold favored stock. I don't generally observe any explanation to forego the development capability of standard stock, or the extra wellbeing given by bonds. For me, it's a half and half that doesn't belong in my portfolio.

In Light of Company Specifics

Each organization has a one of a kind arrangement for development and profit circulations which is reflected in these stock orders.

a. Blue-Chip Stocks

Blue-chip stocks will be stocks of the most significant organizations in the nation. These are generally top notch organizations with long periods of substantial benefits and unfaltering profit installments.

They are likewise probably the most secure stocks. Since the organizations are enormous, stable ventures, they don't have a lot of space to develop.

This typically brings about consistent stock costs, but less upside for financial specialists. Therefore, authentic returns for large organizations have trailed the profits of smaller organizations.

b. Salary Stocks

Salary stocks are as a rule identified with "Blue Chip" stocks.

They are steady organizations that deliver huge profits.

More established individuals who are resigned frequently purchase stocks in these steady pay organizations since it furnishes them with a consistent pay stream as profits (even though I imagine that is an inadequate explanation).

At the point when you join the profit installments with the thankfulness in stock value, these stocks frequently give retirees more cash than they can acquire by putting resources into bonds or other fixed salary ventures. This accompanies a higher risk that the stock cost will fall in a market downturn.

c. Worth Stocks

Worth stocks are the stocks of organizations that typically have at least one of the following:

- Low cost to-profit proportions
- Low cost to-book proportions
- Low cost to-profit proportions
- Low cost to-deals and-income proportions

In other words, they are undervalued when contrasted with other comparable organizations in the market. At times this is a consequence of budgetary issues. Other occasions, it might be because of financial specialist conduct and repetitive patterns.

Development Stocks

Development stocks will be stocks of organizations with benefits that are expanding rapidly. This expansion in benefits is reflected in the rise of its stock cost. These organizations regularly reinvest the gains and deliver next to zero profits to stock proprietors. In doing such, they trust that the development in stock value is sufficient to keep stockholders ready.

Development organizations are frequently innovation focused, and typically either sell an item or spotlight on research and structure.

The vast majority of these organizations experience fast development. Their stock costs regularly become quicker than hidden income, which brings about significant profit/expense (P/E) ratios.

This can proceed for some time.

However, stock costs consistently return to the mean authentic P/E normal, leaving a few speculators to get singed on these stocks.

Development stocks can rise in price rapidly. However, they regularly fall considerably faster.

In light of the size

Market capitalization (market cap) is essentially a method for alluding to the size of an organization in a way that enables you to look at organizations in different enterprises.

You figure market cap by increasing the quantity of outstanding offers by the present stock cost. For instance, if an organization had 100 million shares of typical stock outstanding and a current stock cost of $50 per share, its market cap would be $5 billion (100 million x $50).

Financial specialists, as a rule, arrange organizations under one of these names even though there isn't a general concession to the careful shorts.

- Super cap: Over $200 billion
- Huge cap: Over $10 billion
- Mid-cap: $2 billion
- Little cap: $250 million
- Smaller scale cap: Below $250 million
- Nano-cap: Below $50 million

The size of an organization is significant in stock estimating. Financial specialists frequently talk about contributing in little, mid, or huge cap common assets.

This implies the typical reserve puts resources into organizations of a specific size. There is a stable relationship here between risk and return.

Small organizations are riskier than large organizations since they have fewer assets accessible, haven't set up themselves too in the market place, and may not also be known as the monster stock guarantors. Because of expanded risk, these "little cap" organizations have created more significant yields than "mid cap" or "huge cap" organizations throughout the century. Proceeding with the pattern, "mid cap" stocks have outflanked "huge cap" and "super cap" stocks.

Therefore, numerous financial specialists decide to apportion a more considerable amount of their portfolio to little or mid cap stocks, likewise called a "tilt." Again, this results in marginally more risk.

HOW ARE STOCKS CREATED AND WHY DO THEY EXIST?

Stocks exist for a few reasons, yet among the most significant is the accompanying:

• Stocks enable organizations to raise capital (cash) to transform smart thoughts into practical organizations, which eventually benefits development. Without capitalism and well-working capital markets, the vast majority of the cutting edge products you underestimate wouldn't exist or be accessible to you.

• Stocks give a spot to speculators to conceivably acquire agreeable profits for capital that may enable them to accomplish their budgetary objectives more rapidly than they otherwise could.

• Stocks separate proprietorship from the board, permitting the individuals who have no intrigue, capacity, or time to run a venture even now to take an interest financially. This is done by casting ballot rights, bringing about a progressively effective designation of assets, including human capital.

What Is A Stock Market?

A stock market, which can also be called an equity market, is a system of various financial exchanges, known as the conglomeration of the two merchants and purchasers.

What it isn't, is a physical being. The vendors and purchasers trade stocks. Stocks are securities which exist in a stock trade, albeit some can likewise be traded secretly.

Stock is a term used to symbolize a financial specialist's possession in an organization. The individuals who claim stock are regularly called stockholders or investors. As an investor, a speculator theoretically claims a level of everything the organization possesses or owes.

The organization's gainfulness or scarcity in that department decides if its stock is traded at a sequential cost. While trading of obligation and items has its roots in medieval times, the cutting edge idea of a stock market started in the late sixteenth century.

History

Stock markets were begun when nations in the New World started trading with one another. While many pioneer vendors needed to begin large organizations, this made necessary considerable measures of capital that no single trader could raise alone.

Therefore, gatherings of financial specialists pooled their reserve funds and became colleagues and co-proprietors with singular offers in their organizations to frame business entities. Started by the Dutch, business entities turned into a feasible plan of action for some battling organizations.

In 1602, the Dutch East India Co. started the primary paper shares. This replaceable medium enabled investors to purchase, sell and trade their stock with other investors and investors. In twelfth century France the 'Courretiers de change' assumed the errand of overseeing and controlling rural networks obligation.

This was in the interest of the French banks of that time. This gathering of men traded the obligations and were known as first intermediaries. In the thirteenth century, a typical misguided judgment emerged in Bruges.

Item traders began to meet in a house that was possessed by an honorable man named Van der Beurze, and so later, in 1491, this gathering got known as 'Bruges Beurse'.

This was formalized, and even organized a gathering that had recently been known as a casual gathering. In undeniable reality, those gatherings occurred in a structure in the city of Antwerp that was possessed by Van der Beurze.

Most vendors of that time embraced their trading in the city of Antwerp. This thought spread to the locale of Flanders rapidly, and likewise in neighboring nations, and soon in Ghent and Rotterdam 'Beurzen' were opened.

It was in the thirteenth century in Venice that financiers began to trade in government securities. It was before long banned in 1351, by the legislature of

Venice. The thought behind this was to diminish the expense of Venetian government reserves.

In the large urban areas of Italy, including Pisa, Genoa, Florence and Verona, investors began to trade, again with government securities. This occurred around the fourteenth century.

What enabled this trading to happen was that a duke did not administer these urban areas. They were free states in their very own right. A chosen resident board governed these states.

Organizations and associations in Italy were likewise the first to sell shares on the stock market. It didn't happen until the sixteenth century that organizations in the United Kingdom had the option to sell shares.

Numerous other nations then pursued. The principal business entity was the Dutch East India nation that was framed in 1602. A business entity is an association where stakes can be obtained and sold by investors. An investor may possess an extent of the business relying upon what number offers they buy.

An authentication of possession is given to the investor itemizing the extent of offers held in the organization. The Dutch East India Industry was the first to get fixed capital stock, and so organization stock was regularly traded on Amsterdam Stock Exchange.

It was not long after this happened that other trade pursued, in various subordinates, appeared on the

Amsterdam market. Something known as short selling additionally happened.

This is the place securities that are not at present claimed by anybody are endeavored to be sold. This, however, was before long observed as illicit and was restricted in 1610 by the specialists.

Today, there are stock markets everywhere throughout the world. The most important stock markets are in the United States of America, just as in the United Kingdom, China, Canada, India, Japan, Germany, France, Netherlands and South Korea.

CHAPTER 2:

STOCK MARKET FOR BEGINNERS

Those making their first strides towards learning the nuts and bolts of stock trading ought to approach various wellsprings of value training. Just as with riding a bicycle, experimentation, combined with the capacity to continue squeezing forward, will inevitably prompt achievement.

One incredible preferred position of stock trading lies in the way that the game itself endures forever. Financial specialists have a very long time to create and sharpen their aptitudes.

Methods used twenty years ago are still used today. The game is consistently in full power.

How to Invest in the Stock Market

Are you beginning to consider retirement? Thinking about how you'll have the option to spend your brilliant years in comfort? Putting resources into the stock market is one approach to expand your riches and security. However, it isn't without some genuine risks.

Pursue these tips to get a strong beginning on your monetary future.

STRATEGY 1

Finding out about Stocks

Understand the stock market. To contribute appropriately, you have to understand what the stock market is and how it works. Here's an essential summary of terms and procedures:

Stocks. Likewise alluded to as "offers" or "equity," a stock is a testament that gives the holder part-responsibility for an organization. To fund-raise, an organization discharges shares that the general population can purchase. Each offer speaks to a little level of possession in that organization.

Shareholder. This is an individual who possesses shares in an organization. An investor can hold as few as one offer and upwards of millions. Investors are given votes in the organization and acquire a level of the benefits.

Stock Market. This is the place portions of organizations purchased and sold. It tends to be a physical spot or a virtual market.

The three essential stock markets in the US are the New York Stock Exchange (NYSE), the American Stock Exchange (AMEX), and the National Association of Securities Dealers Automatic Quotation System (NASDAQ). All are open through stockbrokers, both by telephone and on the web.

Acquaint yourself with various types of stocks. There are two primary kinds of stocks: usual and liked.

- **Common stock** is the type of stock generally unmistakable to newcomers. It is an offer in an organization. Underlying stock can give the absolute best yields in contributing yet accompanies the biggest risk.

- **Preferred stock** gives proprietorship as underlying stock does, yet doesn't provide casting a ballot rights. The profits paid out by favored stock are fixed rather than variable like regular stock. Favored stock is a more secure wellspring of profit salary than is regular stock.

- Stocks can likewise be separated into various classes if the organization picks. Ordinarily, an organization will cause one class of offer to have more casting a ballot rights than the other, to ensure that specific gatherings keep up control of the organization.

Find out how stocks rise and fall in esteem. Stocks work as per the law of market interest.

As the demand for a stock increments and a bigger number of individuals are keen on purchasing than selling, the cost of the stock goes up.

This is on the grounds that there is less supply of the stock and each offer turns out to be increasingly significant. Stocks by and large rise in demand as the organization succeeds, and their demand goes down if the organization execution fails.

- Demand is regularly founded on desires for future execution. At the point when financial specialists feel that the organization will perform better sooner rather than later, demand will increment.

- It is difficult to anticipate with any sureness how the general stock market will carry on. This is the reason there is a lot of risk related with this type of speculation.

Get some answers concerning profits. Profits are an advantage paid to investors at the carefulness of the governing body.

- Stable organizations regularly deliver profits to keep financial specialists cheerful when their stock cost doesn't rise a lot.

- Dividends are an extraordinary method to gain "uninvolved" (programmed) pay over an extensive stretch of time.

Understand why you need to buy. Wonder why you need to buy and what you hope to pick up from it.

The stock market can be unpredictable, and an awful day could see you lose a large part of your speculation.

- Good financial specialists buy as long as possible. If you are hoping to trade out immediately, the stock market probably won't be a decent spot to put your cash.

- Don't buy in the event that you are attempting to escape obligation. Ensure any high-premium obligations are dealt with before putting resources into the stock market.

- Successful stock buying requires committed time from the financial specialist. Ask whether you have the opportunity to examine organizations for in any event a couple of hours every day.

Such research is critical. There are many research administrations accessible to do a portion of the leg work for you.

Look online for sites like Scottrade, ShareBuilder, Motley Fool, E-trade, TDAmeritrade, TradeKing, Morningstar, and TheStreet, to give some examples. It is hazardous to pick stocks without first researching them completely.

STRATEGY 2

Picking Stocks to Invest In

Decide your qualities. Since you should do some exploration with regards to which organization to put resources into, concentrate on organizations that you make them work information on. This will make things somewhat more intriguing and connecting as you begin.

- Check nearby organizations, as you may have a greater amount of a chance to discover how their business influences your area.

Think about the general estimation of a stock. You'll have to do some examination and math to decide the estimation of an organization.

You'll before long observe that a one-dollar stock isn't really less expensive than a $40 one. A stock with a genuine worth higher than the recorded value is one that is most likely worth purchasing.

- Since purchasing stock is purchasing part-responsibility for an organization, decide whether it would bode well to purchase the whole organization (if you had the cash).

- Find out how long it would take to take care of your venture from benefits in the event that you purchased the whole organization. Utilize the outcomes to decide whether it is advantageous to put resources into shares.

- Keep at the top of the priority list that benefits can change uncontrollably as markets change. Advances can get outdated, or guidelines could change, rendering an organization's items less important or even futile.

To decide the value of an organization, you should look at a few factors. These include Future Performance, Cash Flow, and Revenue, among numerous others.

- Future Performance. An organization's worth depends to a great extent on projections of future execution. Past execution is significant just as a sign of how the organization will perform later on.

- Cash Flow. As a rule, an organization that has a great deal of advantages and high working costs has less income than a comparable business with less resources and a lower working cost.

Income is money on hand that can be utilized to pay obligation.

- Revenue. Income is one of the main considerations while researching an organization. If two organizations have a similar income, however one has a higher income, that organization will no doubt be worth more.

Make an assorted portfolio. While it is imperative to put resources into what you know, you don't need all your investments tied up in one place.

If something happens to the business that you put resources into, you could lose quite a bit of your interest very soon.

Contribute comprehensively to limit risk of abrupt misfortune.

- Invest in a wide scope of financial divisions. If you are intensely engaged in innovation, think about putting resources into purchaser merchandise, land or any number of other ventures.

- Most speculation specialists discourage placing the entirety of your investable assets into the stock market. Likewise think about bonds, monetary standards, and products.

- Try to make an arrangement of around 20 unique stocks that aren't connected. This should be a reasonable number to monitor while as yet giving a wide exhibit of acquiring openings.

Realize when to purchase. Purchasing at the correct time is basic to fruitful investing.

- Don't purchase everything simultaneously. If the market takes a downturn directly after you buy, you could lose the greater part of your venture.

Rather, spread out your underlying venture to limit the risk each time you purchase.

- Consult a stock diagram when thinking about stock buys. Google and Yahoo both give extensive online stock diagrams, and there are numerous other comparable administrations to browse.

- Check to know whether the stock pattern is rising. This implies the cost has been expanding consistently. Search for stocks that are rising yet not really quickly. Stocks will just go so high, so if a value is climbing quickly, there's a decent possibility that it will level off or drop soon.

- Check the volume of trades. If a stock is finding finding more purchasers, that is an indication of the stock's wellbeing. A rising cost with a declining volume could imply that the cost will drop soon because of the absence of intrigue.

- Find the moving normal of the stock. The moving normal is the normal cost of a stock after some time. In a perfect world, this normal would increment, and the recorded price would be over this normal.

- Avoid unstable stocks. If the value bounces excessively, and there are a ton of spikes in the outline, the stock is likely excessively unsteady to securely put resources into.

Contact a broker when prepared. To purchase stocks, you should use an authorized stockbroker.

There are numerous options to look over, yet they come down to four fundamental decisions. Determine which one will suit your needs the most.

- Online/Discount Broker. Online brokers are basically requesting takers. They give no close to home help and leave the choices of what to purchase and sell up to you. Expenses are generally per-exchange, and they regularly require next to no underlying venture to open a record. The exploration will be up to you.

- Discount Broker with Assistance. This is equivalent to the classification above, except for the broker may give more fundamental research, for example, pamphlets and in-house explore reports. The charge is regularly higher than online simply because of these additional administrations.

- Full-Service Broker. These are the conventional stock brokers who will meet with you and talk about your full monetary circumstance, just as risk examination.

They will help create monetary plans and offer guidance in other money related zones, for example, charges. Full service brokers will be a lot more costly than a rebate broker, yet many offer tremendous advantages.

- Money Manager. A cash director assumes full responsibility for your accounts. Their customers are regularly those with high salaries, and the standard least record is $100,000 or more.

And hold great stocks. Selling stocks when they ascend in cost is a specific method to move no place quick. Practice restraint and hold strong stocks except if you're edgy to raise money.

Great stocks can bring about large settlements as time goes on.

- If you purchase and sell over and over, quite a bit of your benefit will go to commissions for brokers, and your increases will endure.

- "Day trading" is stacked against newcomers, since they trade against prepared experts and PC programs intended to purchase and sell at ideal minutes.

- Instead, clutch stocks of organizations that are strong and developing. If your stocks deliver profits, reinvest them to build your gaining potential.

Add to your portfolio as you go. When your portfolio is built up, return to it now and again and roll out suitable improvements.

- Move cash out of areas that aren't performing admirably and put more in areas that are seeing more noteworthy returns.

- Add more ventures with surplus assets as they become accessible to keep expanding.

Realize when to sell. In a perfect world, you need to sell a stock when it arrives at the worth you decided when exploring the organization, and when the worth isn't relied upon to rise significantly more.

- If your stock has not met the actual worth and doesn't resemble it will sell it, mainly if the value falls beneath the moving normal. This is ordinarily observed as the "last possibility" to dispose of a stock before it plunges too low. Expect to pay a charge for each exchange you make.

Brokers make their cash charging you for each time you purchase or sell a stock. You have to realize this charge going in, yet you additionally need to make it evident to your broker your satisfactory degree of trading.

A few brokers will attempt to sucker in tenderfoot financial specialists with high-commission stocks and numerous trades to get more cash-flow.

- If you have a huge record and plan on a visit or forceful trades, you may search for a commission-based file, where the broker gets a level of your portfolio rather than an expense for every trade.

- If your broker is rolling out regular improvements and trades, known as "beating," they might be attempting to raise their bonus. Any trading that eats into your chief ought to be red-hailed.

Anticipate that your broker should solicit your satisfactory level of risk. Your risk resilience decides how much speculation the broker will take. Stocks are betting, and there are both sure things and long-shots.

Your broker will need direction on where to control the portfolio, because of your money related needs:

- Younger speculators can go for high-risk ventures. Stocks are a long-term game, and any busts presently will more than likely be corrected with later blasts. You have the opportunity to bear the cost of the risk.
- Middle-matured financial specialists should find some harmony among sheltered and risky stocks.
- Low-risk records will concentrate on things with lower benefits. These are good for more established speculations which couldn't manage an abrupt loss of cash close to retirement, or the individuals who need moderate, solid development.

Anticipate that most expert financial specialists should pick edge accounts, not money accounts. There are two fundamental venture account options - money and money/edge accounts.

Money accounts must have a store accessible to make a trade- - the cash must be on hand. Edge accounts enable you to obtain some money from the brokerage firm to buy stocks.

This credit depends on the regular benefit of the stock.

- Cash accounts are more secure, yet return far less benefit. You know precisely where all your cash is, and whose cash it is.

- Margin accounts put you into an obligation. However, loan fees are far lower than at a bank. Since they get more cash-flow accessible to you, you stand to procure more cash. Some higher-risk trades are just available on edge accounts.

Anticipate that the broker should decide your assessment status dependent on your money related needs.

It is okay to say that you are in the stock game to make a benefit at this moment, or for retirement? Contingent upon how you group your portfolio, your broker can get you conceivably lower charge rates.

- Standard brokerage records can be swapped, taken out, and altered on the fly. They can be short or long haul ventures or a touch of both. They are completely burdened.

- Retirement accounts, similar to IRAs, cover a lot of lower charges. However, you can remove the cash from them at a particular age, or risk losing quite a bit of your benefit.

- A proficient trader would ordinarily have the two sorts of records. However, this requires a great deal of forthright cash.

Anticipate that the gathering should end with a solicitation for your venture cash. Most brokers will give you about fourteen days to give them money.

You can cut a check, which generally would take about seven days to get cleared. In case you're in a rush, hope to get a steering number and guidelines to wire your cash over.

- Professional speculators continuously put in a safe spot explicit records for ventures. They don't connect their speculation cash to reserve funds or checking account.

Expect an expert broker frequently utilizes calculation based trading.

The stock market isn't what it used to be. Experts presently have mines of information and PC projects to filter through them, settling on split-second trading choices for your venture that you could once in a while make alone.

This is the reason, if you have the cash, full-scale brokers frequently turn the most elevated benefits.

- That stated, the budgetary accident of 2007 was somewhat due to a wrecked calculation that financial specialists utilized yet didn't understand.[9]

Anticipate that an expert should put resources into things other than stock.

While putting resources into the stock market might be the objective, an expert financial specialist knows not to place the entirety of their cash in one container. These, including stocks, fall under the full meaning of a "security."

- CDs, or Certificates of Deposit, are investment accounts that develop at a specific date, so, all things considered, you get a little benefit. They can go from one month to five years.

- Bonds are advances that your award, typically to the administration, that must be taken care of with intrigue. They are protected, reliable ventures that for the most part, outpace swelling.

- Expect a broker to put resources into "reserves," or pre-made assortments of stocks. Assets are made either by a brokerage firm or an outside organization.

- Essentially, they enable different speculators to risk together by all paying together for a more significant portfolio, and in this way more benefit as there is usually a supervisor of the assets who purchases and sells stocks within it.

While they are typically beneficial, you must be alright with another person handling your cash with little control on your end.

CHAPTER 3:

STOCK MARKETING STRATEGIES

For some recently settled investors, the possibility of effectively trading in the markets can be scary. It is practically unthinkable not to be overpowered by the sheer assortment of venture stages, resources and dialect that are presently an inalienable component of current investing.

Despite the fact that acing the markets may take long periods of patient investigation and practice, there is an assortment of moderately precise stock trading techniques that you can start utilizing immediately.

These incorporate development in investing, esteem investing, shared reserve venture and IRA speculations, among others. In every situation, you ought to have the option to make well-informed, well-investigated trading choices utilizing market trading techniques that assure the ideal possibilities for a rewarding return.

Tips

Finding the ideal market trading techniques will, to a great extent, rely upon your present experience level and investing objectives.

Development investing, esteem investing, shared assets and IRAs are almighty components of current trading procedures.

Development Investing and Stock Trading

As a rule, development investing is characterized as the distinguishing proof of organizations which, through careful research, are viewed as capable of becoming quicker than the average record rate.

The essential goal of development investing is the best conceivable increment in the financial specialist's capital increases.

In numerous situations, the organizations distinguished in this methodology are assessed dependent on five parameters, those being:

1.   They have exhibited a past filled with better than expected income.

2.   Whether or not the organisation's forward income development, or its foreseen profit for the next quarter, matches financial specialist desires.

3.   The viability of the board at controlling expenses while boosting income.

4.   The current style of oversight conveyed by the executives.

5.   The probability that the benefit will rise twofold inside five years.

Assessing an organization dependent on these five parameters will enable you to decide if it would as a suitable component of a development venture methodology.

Development Investing and Emerging Companies

Another feature of modern day development investing is particular interest in smaller, rising organizations whose current offer cost may not mirror the genuine capability of the organization.

For instance, if a speculator accepts that a generally small company traded on an open market organization can become hugely dependent on their items and administrations, they would almost certainly qualify as a reasonable candidate for development investing.

Remember, however, that this specific component of the trading methodology can be risky for a number of reasons.

Especially in circumstances where an organization presently can't seem to convey the item or administration being referred to, it is altogether conceivable that the organization could come up short and the stock would be downgraded, bringing about a complete loss of speculation reserves.

It is also very critical to take note that smaller organizations will commonly have a considerably lower trading volume than large cap stocks. Along these lines, the stock will be exposed to expanded unpredictability and might be more diligently to sell if costs begin to decay quickly.

Understanding Value Investing

Mainly, financial specialists try to buy stocks whose present deal cost is beneath what the speculators consider to be its intrinsic worth.

From numerous points of view, esteem investing is the same as shopping deals. In the wake of accessible auditing stocks, financial specialists search out determinations which, for reasons unknown, are right now underestimated.

A stock may become underestimated for an assortment of reasons. For instance, a general market downturn because of lost speculator certainty could push the deal cost of a stock beneath its true worth.

Other issues, for example, frustrating quarterly profit reports or media scandals, could likewise incidentally push the cost of stock underneath its present worth.

It is in times like these where esteem speculators buy the stock being referred to and hold the advantage until its deal value comes back to or surpasses its inherent worth.

Significant Data Points for Value Investing

Financial specialists primarily depend on a stock's cost to-income proportion, additionally alluded to as the P/E proportion, and its profit yield. As communicated in the term itself, the P/E proportion is a quantitative estimation of the value a stock is presently selling for compared with the particular profit per share announced every year by the organization.

Thus, for instance, if a stock has a P/E proportion of 10, this implies the present cost of the stock is multiple times more noteworthy than the income per single portion of stock the organization has delivered.

When in doubt, financial specialists look for the lowest conceivable P/E proportion while choosing likely stock targets.

This is because of the way that stocks with high P/E proportions may as of now be exaggerated, which would then likely prompt a value revision rather than development.

A stock is generally viewed as an attractive venture open door for financial specialists if its P/E proportion is beneath 10.

Understanding Earnings Yield

Straightforwardly identified with the P/E proportion of a stock is its income yield. Income yield is characterized as the estimation of the profit per portion of an organization for the latest year time frame communicated as a partial measure of the present market cost of the stock.

The income yield of a stock is the precise reverse of its profit multiplier.

For instance, think about the accompanying: An organization has a year profit for each offer estimation of $3.75 per share. The present estimation of the stock is $17. To ascertain the income yield, utilize the accompanying condition:

(income per share) 3.75/(current market value) 17 = 0.22.

For esteem speculators, the higher the profit yield, the more alluring the stock becomes as a potential venture.

Starting Mutual Fund Investing

For those speculators who are reluctant about trading single stocks, a natural reserve might be one of the better market trading methodologies accessible.

By definition, a typical store is an aggregate pool of cash that is effectively regulated by a reserve supervisor and is put resources into different stocks, securities and other funds as a component of an income age procedure.

A significant early differentiation to be made is that a typical reserve doesn't need to be made solely out of stocks. A considerable lot of the best common assets in presence today convey an exceptionally expanded portfolio to support against different types of market choppiness. There are two essential types of shared supports open to financial specialists today: shut finished assets and open-finished assets. These two marks help characterize how speculators buy partakes in the store and how precisely these offers pick up or lose an incentive after some time. Understanding this differentiation will help guarantee that you know precisely how your cash is being spent.

Open-Ended versus Shut Ended Mutual Funds

If you are anticipating buying a stake in a common reserve, you might be amazed to discover that a portion of these offers are not accessible in the stock market.

This is because of the way that open-finished assets have a virtually boundless number of offers accessible and are traded outside of the stock market. A reserve director running an open-finished store can consent to take on as a lot of capital from speculators as they feel confident they can sensibly oversee.

They gather this capital through the issuance of offers, which are straightforwardly bought from the store itself. In light of this thought, the costs of portions of an open-finished store are not presented to market movement similarly that standard stocks are.

An open-finished reserve's offer value is fixed for a trading day, implying that offers can be bought for the day at the built up cost. Changes in share cost will be an immediate impression of the net asset value, or NAV, of the reserve itself. When the value of the open-finished offer is built up, singular propositions can't be bought at some other cost during the trading session.

Valuing Closed-Ended Mutual Funds

The valuing techniques utilized for shut-finished assets vary enormously from that of open-finished assets, due principally to the way that there are just a fixed number of shut-finished offers accessible.

These offers exist in limited inventory and are traded on stock trades simply like some other stock. Offers are first made to financial specialists as a component of the first sale of stock, or IPO, similarly as they would be with some other stock.

When the offers have been made and offered through the IPO, no extra offers can be made.

Given the way that these offers a trade in the open marketplace, the cost of a shut-finished reserve share is impacted by speculator assessment the same amount of for what it's worth by the genuine estimation of the advantages in the store itself.

Given the way that shut-finished store shares are traded in people in general markets, the cost of these offers can vacillate fundamentally all through a solitary trading day.

Fluctuating degrees of organic market ordinarily bring about portions of shut finished subsidizes trading above or beneath the net resource estimation of the reserve itself.

Essentials of Investing in IRAs

Most market specialists exhort that recently settled financial specialists unmistakably characterize their speculation objectives before they start trading in the markets.

The purposes behind this are moderately straightforward: if a speculator recognizes what their ideal outcome is before they start trading, certain venture stages might be undeniably progressively helpful for contacting them.

As an extraordinary model, think about the subject of retirement. Many working grown-ups put resources into the market so as to help make a "savings" that they can use to during retirement — one of the best.

Known market stages that are straightforwardly custom fitted to these objectives is an individual retirement account or IRA.

IRAs are one of a kind in the way that they offer explicit assessment preferences to financial specialists in return for keeping their assets contributed to an all-inclusive timeframe.

Roth IRAs versus Traditional IRAs

Any exchange of IRAs will without a doubt think about conventional IRAs and Roth IRA plans. In the two situations, financial specialists can store assets up to a governmentally mandated point of confinement every year.

After arriving at the age of 59 1/2, account proprietors can start pulling back assets from their IRA. It is during this dispersion procedure that the unmistakable contrasts between Roth IRAs and customary IRAs develop.

With a conventional IRA, people can absolve the pay they place in the IRA from their yearly assessment announcing. These assets can be stored straightforwardly in the IRA and are not revealed as pay on that year's tax form.

However, during the appropriation time frame, withdrawals from the record will be taxed at ordinary annual expense rates.

This procedure is not quite the same as the Roth IRA, due in enormous part to the way that people are required to pay the charge on their Roth IRA commitments at the time the speculation is made. In return, they are not required to pay charge during the withdrawal procedure.

Given the way that the assets in their record may become hugely over the term of the record, an underlying duty installment might be altogether not exactly the assessment on withdrawal at a later point.

Dynamic Trading Strategies

Dynamic trading is the demonstration of purchasing and undercutting securities dependent on term developments to benefit from the value developments on a transient stock diagram.

The mindset related to a functioning trading methodology varies from the long haul, purchase-and-hold technique found among aloof or listed speculators. Dynamic traders accept that transient development and capturing the market pattern are the place the benefits are made.

Dynamic trading is a procedure that includes 'beating the market' through recognizing and timing beneficial trades, frequently for short holding periods.

Inside dynamic trading, there are a few general techniques that can be utilized.

Day trading, position trading, swing trading, as well as scalping are four well known dynamic trading approaches.

1. DAY TRADING

Day trading is maybe the most notable dynamic trading style. It's regularly viewed as a nom de plume dynamic trading itself. Day trading, as its name infers, is the strategy for purchasing and selling securities around the same time.

Positions are finished off around the same time they are taken, and no position is held medium-term. Generally, day trading is finished by proficient traders, for example, masters or market producers.

However, electronic trading has opened this up to fledgling traders.

2. POSITION TRADING

Some consider position trading to be a purchase-and-hold procedure and not dynamic trading. However, position trading, when done by a propelled trader, can be a type of active trading.

Position trading utilizes longer term diagrams – anytime from day by day to month to month – in blend with other strategies to decide the pattern of the present market bearing.

This kind of trade may keep going for a few days to half a month and at times longer, contingent upon the pattern.

Pattern traders search for progressive higher highs or lower highs to decide the pattern of security. By bouncing on and riding the "wave," pattern traders plan to profit by both the up and drawback of market developments.

Pattern traders hope to decide the bearing of the market, yet they don't attempt to figure any value levels. Ordinarily, pattern traders hop on the pattern after it has set up itself, and when the pattern breaks, they, as a rule, leave the position.

This implies in times of high market unpredictability, pattern trading is progressively troublesome, and its positions are commonly diminished.

3. SWING TRADING

At the point when a pattern breaks, swing traders regularly get in the game. Toward the finish of a pattern, there is typically some value unpredictability as the new pattern attempts to build up itself. Swing traders purchase or sell as that value instability sets in. Swing trades are typically held for over a day yet for a shorter time than pattern trades. Swing traders frequently make a lot of trading rules dependent on specialized or basic investigation.

These trading rules or calculations are intended to distinguish when to purchase and sell a security.

While a swing-trading calculation doesn't need to be correct and foresee the pinnacle or valley of a value move, it needs a market that moves toward some path. A range-bound or sideways market is dangerous for swing traders.

4. SCALPING

Scalping is perhaps the fastest system utilized by dynamic traders. It incorporates abusing different value holes brought about by offer ask spreads and request streams.

The methodology, for the most part, works by making the spread or purchasing at the offer cost and selling at the request that value gets the distinction between the two value focuses.

Hawkers endeavor to hold their situations for a brief period, hence diminishing the risk related to the system.

Furthermore, a hawker doesn't attempt to misuse huge moves or move high volumes. Rather, they attempt to exploit little moves that happen now and again and move smaller volumes all the more frequently.

Since the degree of benefits per trade is small, hawkers search for increasingly fluid markets to expand the recurrence of their trades.

And not at all like swing traders, hawkers like calm markets that aren't inclined to abrupt value developments so they can possibly make the spread over and over on a similar offer/ask costs.

Costs Inherent With Trading Strategies

There's an explanation dynamic that trading systems were once just utilized by proficient traders. Having an in-house brokerage house does not always lessen the expenses related to high-recurrence trading, however, it guarantees better trade execution.

Lower commissions and better execution are two components that improve the benefit capability of the procedures. Huge equipment and programming buys are ordinarily required to effectively actualize these procedures. Notwithstanding continuous market information, these costs make dynamic trading to some degree restrictive, but achievable, for the individual trader. This is the reason inactive and listed systems that take a purchase-and-hold position, offer lower expenses and trading costs, just as lower assessable occasions in case of selling a beneficial position. Inactive methodologies can't beat the market since they hold the expansive market list. Dynamic traders look for 'alpha', with the expectation that trading benefits will surpass expenses and make for a fruitful lengthy haul procedure.

Tips

1. Look for a coach/gathering of fruitful traders who can accelerate your instruction.

2. Never intend to make a couple of pennies an offer on any stock trade

3. Maintain a strategic distance from FOMO (fear of missing out) no matter what. FOMO can and will prompt settling on poor choices.

It makes no difference if you pass up something. Once more, there are such huge numbers of prospects. You will gain from all of them, and be better arranged for the future.

4. Trade the genuine stock.

5. You don't need to trade each day. Hold on for the best arrangements.

CHAPTER 4:

STOCK MARKETING ANALYSIS

WHAT IS A STOCK MARKET ANALYSIS?

The stock market investigation empowers speculators to distinguish the inherent worth of security even before investing in it. All stock market tips are detailed after intensive research by a specialist.

Stock experts attempt to discover the action of an instrument/division/market in future.

By utilizing stock investigation, financial specialists and traders land at equity purchasing and selling choices. Contemplating and assessing past and current information encourages financial specialists and traders to increase an edge in the markets to settle on educated choices.

Crucial Research and Technical Research are two kinds of research used to initially dissect and then worth security.

UNDERSTANDING STOCK ANALYSIS

The stock examination is a technique for speculators and traders to settle on purchasing and selling choices. By examining and assessing past and current information, speculators and traders endeavor to increase an edge in the markets by settling on educated choices.

WHAT IS FUNDAMENTAL ANALYSIS?

This technique expects to assess the estimation of the basic organization. It considers the characteristic estimation of the offer remembering the monetary conditions and the business alongside the organization's money related condition and the executive's execution.

An essential investigator would look at the monetary record, the benefit and misfortune articulation, money related proportions and other information that could be utilized to foresee the eventual fate of an organization.

In other words, crucial offer market investigation is tied in with utilizing genuine information to assess a stock's worth. The strategy utilizes incomes, profit, future development, return on equity, overall revenues and other information to decide an organization's fundamental worth and potential for future development.

The fundamental conviction is that as the organization develops so will the estimation of the offer increment. This will profit the financial specialist over the long haul.

What is an exaggerated stock or an underestimated stock?

When you look at the monetary record and other budgetary subtleties, you use proportions to contrast the financials and the cost of the stock.

This understands how much a financial specialist is truly paying in correlation with the organization's development. The most widely recognized proportion utilized is the Price-to-Earnings or P/E proportion.

This is processed by separating the offer cost with the organization's profit per share.

If the offer cost in correlation with its income per share is not as much as industry normal, then the stock is said to be underestimated.

This implies the stock is selling at a much lower cost than what it is really worth.

Conversely, an exaggerated stock is the place the speculator is paying more for all money the organization gets. This implies the stock's value surpasses its inherent worth.

This frequently happens when financial specialists anticipate that the organization should do well later on.

A high P/E in connection to the past P/E proportion of a similar stock may show an exaggerated condition, or a high P/E in connection to peer stocks may likewise demonstrate an exaggerated stock.

However, as a financial specialist, you must be cautious. Analyze the key estimation of the stock with its notable qualities. If there is an abrupt increment in valuation, there are high possibilities that the cost may tumble to address the mispricing.

In the event of an abrupt fall in value, check for any recent news about the organization. Almost certainly, some new factor may have developed that might affect the organization's benefits.

Since the P/E is processed utilizing the profit per share for the year passed by, it is known as a trailing P/E. This is certifiably not an ideal method to understand the stock's worth.

Consequently, examiners regularly utilize the forward P/E, where the assessed income per share for the present or another year is utilized.

WHAT IS TECHNICAL ANALYSIS?

In contrast to the major investigation, the specialized examination has nothing to do with the monetary presentation of the basic organization. In this technique, the examiner basically ponders the pattern in the offer costs.

The hidden supposition will be that market costs are a component of the organic market for the stock, which, thus, mirrors the estimation of the organization. This technique additionally accepts that authentic value patterns are a sign of things to come to execution.

Along these lines, rather than evaluating the strength of the organization by depending on its fiscal reports, it depends upon market patterns to anticipate how security will perform.

Examiners attempt to take advantage of the force that develops after some time in the market or a stock.

A specialized investigation is regularly utilized by momentary speculators and traders, and occasionally by long haul financial specialists, who incline toward key examination.

Specialized examiners peruse and make diagrams of costs. Some normal specialized offer market investigation measures are the day-moving midpoints (DMAs), Bollinger bands, Relative Strength Indices (RSI), and so on.

INVESTING PHILOSOPHIES

So now you think about stock market examination strategies. How does that truly enable you to contribute? These investing ways of thinking will allow you to understand.

WHAT DOES WORTH INVESTING MEAN?

Worth investing is a speculation style, which supports great stocks at incredible costs over extraordinary stocks at great. Thus, it is frequently alluded to as 'cost is driven investing'.

A worth speculator will purchase stocks that might be underestimated by the market, and keep away from stocks that he accepts the market is exaggerating. Warren Buffett, one of the world's best-known venture specialists, puts stock in esteem investing.

For instance, if stock of an organization developing at 10% is selling at $100 with a P/E proportion of 10 and stock of another organization that likewise develops at 10% is selling at $150 with a P/E proportion of 15, the worth financial specialist would choose the first stock over the second.

This is on the grounds that the first stock is underestimated in correlation with the second.

Worth speculators see the potential in the stocks of organizations with sound budget reports that they accept the market has underestimated.

They accept the market consistently goes overboard to great and terrible news, causing stock value developments to not move in tandem with long haul essentials. Hence, they are consistently on the chase for underestimated organizations.

Worth financial specialists benefit by taking a situation on an underestimated stock (at an emptied cost) and then profit by selling the stock when the market revises its value later.

Worth speculators don't attempt to anticipate what direction financing costs are going or the bearing of the market and the economy for the time being.

They take a gander at a stock's present valuations and contrast them with their recorded range.

In other words, they get the stocks as juveniles and cash in on them when they are esteemed right in the markets.

For instance, say a specific stock's P/E proportion has run between a low of 20 and a high of 60 in recent years, financial specialists would consider purchasing the stock if its present P/E is around 30 or less.

Once obtained, they would hold the stock until its P/E rose to the 50-60 area before they think about selling it. If they anticipate further development, later on, they may keep on holding.

WHAT IS CONTRARIAN PHILOSOPHY?

As the name recommends, the contrarian philosophy proposes trading against the market slant. This implies you purchase stocks when they are out of support in the market place and maintaining a strategic distance from stocks that everybody is purchasing.

They then sell these stocks when they restore the support.

Contrarians have faith in removing preferences that emerge from impermanent mishaps or negative news that has made a stock's value decay.

A straightforward case of the contrarian philosophy would purchase umbrellas in the winter at a modest rate and selling them during stormy days. Worth investing is a sort of contrarian philosophy.

HOW TO PLACE CONTRARIAN TRADES
If you are a contrarian trader:

• Conduct stock market examination. Discover stocks with low P/E proportions.

• Once you do that, contrast and recorded P/E proportions and offer costs.

• Read up about the organization, its budgetary exhibition and future viewpoint. If you feel that the organization is innately commendable, select the stock.

• Wait at the costs to decrease. Purchase at lows.

• You could likewise look at market pointers like common store money positions, and put/call proportions and venture warning feelings. Common subsidizes hold a few of their benefits as money.

A more prominent money holding proposes that shared assets are bearish, while a low money holding implies common assets are investing cash in the markets.

This implies they are bullish. When you understand this, take a precisely inverse position. Sell when MFs are purchasing and purchase when they are selling.

• A put option is a consent to sell later on in the subordinates market, while a call option is a point at which you consent to purchase later on.

The put/call proportion causes you to understand the extent of put options and call options. The higher this proportion, the more prominent the put options, and the other way around.

• An increment in put options proposes that the market is bearish, while demand for call options implies the market is bullish. As a contrarian trader, you ought to plan in like manner.

• Investment warnings are given by numerous brokerage firms and venture banks, which consistently lead an examination of individual stocks, businesses and the general economy. A positive proposal frequently prompts an expansion in share cost as financial specialists purchase the stock. Contrarian traders could purchase when negative venture warnings are given, and sell after positive proposals.

Why is the Stock Market Analysis significant?

Playing out exploration before making speculation is an absolute necessity. It is simply after intensive research that you can make a few suppositions into the worth and future exhibition of a venture.

Regardless of whether you are following stock trading tips, it is good to do some exploration, just to guarantee that you are making a speculation that is relied upon to get you most extreme returns.

At the point when you put resources into equity, you buy a few segments of a business hoping to profit upon increment in the estimation of the business.

Prior to purchasing anything, be it a vehicle or telephone, you do some level of research about its exhibition and quality. A venture is the same.

It is your well deserved cash that you are going to contribute, so you should have reasonable information on what you are investing in.

There are two essential sorts of stock examination: crucial investigation and specialized examination.

PRINCIPAL ANALYSIS
The principal examination focuses on information from sources, including monetary records, financial reports, organization resources, and market share.

To direct key examination on an open organization or part, speculators and experts normally break down the measurements on an organization's fiscal reports – monetary record, pay proclamation, income explanation, and commentaries.

These announcements are discharged to general society as a 10-Q or 10-K report through the database framework, EDGAR, which is directed by the US Securities and Exchange Commission (SEC).

Likewise, the income report discharged by an organization during its quarterly income public statement is dissected by financial specialists who hope to find out how much incomes, costs, and benefits an organization made.

When running a stock investigation on an organization's budget summaries, an expert will normally be checking for the proportion of an organization's benefit, liquidity, dissolvability, productivity, development direction, and influence.

Various proportions can be utilized to decide how solid an organization is. For instance, the present proportion and snappy proportion are utilized to evaluate whether an organization will have the option to pay its transient liabilities with its accessible current resources.

The equation for the current proportion is determined by dividing current resources by current liabilities, figures that can be gotten from the monetary record. Despite the fact that there is no such thing as a perfect current proportion, a proportion under one could show to the stock expert that the organization is in poor money related wellbeing and will most likely be unable to cover its momentary obligation commitments when they come due.

Looking at the asset report still, a stock expert might need to realize the present obligation levels taken on by an organization.

For this situation, a stock expert may utilize the obligation proportion, which is determined by dividing complete liabilities by absolute resources.

An obligation proportion over one ordinarily implies that an organization has more obligations than resources.

For this situation, if the organization has a high level of influence, a stock examiner may reason that an ascent in loan fees may build the organization's probability of going into default.

The stock investigation includes contrasting an organization's present budget report with its fiscal summaries in earlier years to give a financial specialist a feeling of whether the organization is developing, stable, or breaking down.

The budget summary of an organization can likewise be contrasted with that of at least one other organizations inside a similar industry.

A stock examiner might be hoping to think about the working net revenue of two contending organizations, by taking a gander at their pay articulations. The working net revenue is a metric that shows how much income is left after working costs have been paid and what extent of income is left to take care of non-working expenses and is determined as working salary divided by income.

An organization with a working edge of 0.30 will be looked on better than one with an edge of 0.03. A 0.30 working edge implies that for each dollar of income, an organization has 30 pennies left in the wake of working expenses have been secured. In other words, the organization utilizes 70 pennies out of each dollar in net deals to pay for its variable or working expenses.

Which key markers are utilized in Fundamental Research?

Monetary proportions structure the mainstays of principal examine. Some of them are as per the following:

PROFIT FOR EQUITY (ROE)

Profit for Equity educates you regarding how much does an organization procure on investors' equity. It gives you data separated from a straightforward benefit figure. It shows whether the tasks of the organization are effective or not.

Profit For Equity = [(Income − Preference Dividend)/(Average Shareholders' Equity)]*100

While searching for this measurement, a perfect ROE is one which is reliable, high and expanding. ROE of one organization can be contrasted and its own past exhibition and with the execution of other organizations inside a similar industry. You may utilize it regardless of the sort of industry.

OBLIGATION EQUITY RATIO (DER)

Obligation Equity Ratio shows the extent of benefits which is being utilized to fund the advantages of the organization.

It demonstrates how much assets have been given by the borrowers and proprietors of the organization. This proportion can be communicated in numbers and in rate.

Obligation Equity (D/E) Ratio = Total Debt/Total Equity

While searching for an obligation equity proportion, go for the ones which are lower than others and are diminishing in a predictable way.

You can look at D/E of one organization with its own past presentation and with the execution of other organizations inside a similar industry.

You may use it to examine execution of capital escalated enterprises like capital products, metals, oil and gas.

PROFIT PER SHARE (EPS)
Profit per Share is one such valuable measure which the speculators search for constantly. It shows the measure of cash which the organization is acquiring on each offer. EPS of an organization needs to rise in a steady way to show prevalent administration execution.

Profit per Share = (Net Income – Preference Dividend)/Weighted Average Number of Shares Outstanding

EPS of one organization can be contrasted and its past presentation with that of other organizations in a similar industry.

It tends to be utilized to determine what part of benefit the company is allocating to all outstanding shares.

Investors normally go to businesses that have steadily rising earnings per share. Comparing output across sectors can be conveniently utilized.

COST TO EARNINGS RATIO (CER)

Cost to Earnings Ratio thinks about the present market cost of the offer with the profit per share.

It discloses to you the value which the financial specialists are eager to pay for the offer contingent upon the present income.

Cost to Earnings Ratio = Current Share Price/Earnings per Share

This proportion likewise demonstrates the number of years that will be required to get back the underlying contributed capital by method for returns. You have to search for stocks which have a low cost to profit proportion.

You can look at P/E proportion of an organization with its past presentation and likewise with other organizations in a similar industry.

In a perfect world, this proportion is reasonable to examine execution of organizations present in FMCG, pharmaceutical and innovation area.

SPECIALIZED ANALYSIS

The second technique for stock examination is a specialized investigation. Specialized investigation centers around the investigation of past market activity to foresee future value development.

Specialized investigators examine the budgetary market all in all and are fundamentally worried about cost and volume, just as the demand and supply factors that move the market.

Diagrams are a key device for specialized experts as they show a graphical delineation of a stock's pattern inside an expressed timespan. For instance, utilizing a diagram, a specialized investigator may stamp certain regions as a help or obstruction level.

The help levels are set apart by past lows underneath the present trading cost, and the obstruction markers are put at past highs over the present market cost of the stock.

A break beneath the help level would show a bearish pattern to the stock expert, while a break over the obstruction level would take on a bullish viewpoint.

The specialized stock examination is viable just when organic market powers impact the value pattern broke down.

When outside variables are associated with a value development, examining stocks utilizing specialized examination may not be fruitful.

Instances of components, other than the organic market that can influence a stock value to incorporate stock parts, mergers, profit declarations, a legal claim, demise of an organization's CEO, a fear based oppressor assault, bookkeeping scandals, change of the executives, and money related approach changes, and so on.

Both crucial and specialized examination should be possible, autonomously or together. A few experts utilize the two strategies for examination, while others stick to one.

Either way, utilizing stock examination to vet stocks, segments, and the market is a significant technique for making the best speculation system for one's portfolio.

What is Specialized Research?

Specialized research identifies with the investigation of past stock costs to foresee the pattern of costs in future. It shows you the course of development of the offer costs.

With the assistance of specialized research, you can distinguish whether there will be sharp rise or fall in the cost of the offer. It isn't reliant on late news or occasions which have just been joined in the cost of the offer.

As the stock costs are subject to financial specialist brain science which continues changing as indicated by news and occasions, specialized research accentuates the utilization of Stop misfortunes.

It will spare financial specialists from enduring a major misfortune in future. Specialized research gives important outcomes just for stocks which are high in demand and traded in colossal volumes.

Specialized research utilizes various kinds of diagrams like a bar graph, candlestick outline; to understand the example of stock costs

Every day graphs are utilized by momentary traders to look at the prompt development in the stock costs.

The week after week/month to month diagrams are utilized by medium/long haul traders to find out the probability to gain higher more over the long haul.

CHAPTER 5:

HOW TO START IN THE STOCK MARKET WITH $500

Everyone realizes they ought to put something aside in preparation for retirement. In any case, when you're youthful, it can appear as though that day is well far off, and you have a lot of time.

In addition, maybe you're simply beginning a vocation, you probably won't have a great deal of additional cash to spare or contribute for your future.

However, you needn't bother with thousands of dollars to begin investing. Online brokers and portable applications make it conceivable to put resources into the stock market, regardless of whether you can just afford a couple of pennies daily.

Visit a few distinctive miniaturized scale investing apps. There are various venture apps accessible for both Android and iOS cellphones.

A large number of these apps likewise have a full site with extra speculation highlights you won't discover on the app.

- Some apps require a base store to open your record or expect you to make a guarantee to invest a certain amount of cash every month. Others, for example, Acorns, have a gather together element where the app gathers together your regular buys to the closest dollar and contributes that change for you.

- The best app for you may rely upon how a lot of cash you have accessible to contribute and whether you need to begin investing immediately. For instance, Robinhood offers free stock trades, yet you can't purchase fragmentary portions of stock – just full shares.

Compute the genuine expense of any charges. Numerous miniaturized scale investing applications charge moderately little level expenses every month, regularly under $5.

However, contingent upon how much you intend to contribute, that little level charge could really speak to a huge level of the cash you have invested.

- For model, if your app charges a month to month administration expense of $1, and you contribute $10 per month, that adds up to a 10 percent charge.

Most online brokers charge fundamentally lower expenses than that, despite the fact that they may have higher least equalization or commitment necessities.

Set up your investing account. Download the app you need to set up your record directly from your cellphone. The procedure fluctuates among the diverse apps. At any rate, you'll have to give some individual data. You'll likely additionally need to interface your bank account.

- After you set up your record, the app may walk you through some fundamental data about speculation methodology and how the stock market works.

A considerable lot of these assets will be accessible for you to look at later if you need a boost.

Tip: Look for any advancements before you open your record. Numerous apps offer arrangements for new financial specialists, for example, referral rewards or no charges for the initial scarcely any months.

Pick your record type and venture methodology. Smaller scale investing apps commonly give a scope of expansive portfolio portrayals and enable you to pick one. You'll likewise likely need to respond to inquiries regarding whether you need to have the option to get to your cash right away.

- If you're setting up a retirement account, you'll need to choose whether you need to pay charges on pay from those records now, or have those assessments conceded until you really get to the cash.

Set up week by week or month to month commitments. When you've linked your financial balance to your app, you can set up programmed installments every week or every month. Some applications have a base required contribution.

- Look at your spending limit and decide how much cash you can stand to put towards ventures. Remember this isn't cash you'll have the option to get to promptly if you need it.

Look at a few changed online brokers. Look at expenses and charges, just as the broker's interface.

In the event that having the option to get to your record from your telephone is significant, look at their versatile application as well.

- The broker's site ought to be easy to explore, with a moderately natural interface.

- If you have thoughts of the sorts of stock you need to put resources into, ensure the broker offers that stock for procurement.

Check the base record store necessity. In a situation that you don't have a great deal of cash, the base record store necessity might be the greatest factor deciding which broker you pick.

Luckily, there are numerous online brokers with low least equalization necessities. Some even enable you to open your record with no underlying store.

- For model, Betterment enables you to open a record with a zero equalization, and likewise doesn't require a base parity to keep up your record. TD Ameritrade likewise has no base introductory store necessity.

- Charles Schwab and others have a base equalization necessity of $1,000, yet it tends to be postponed if you set up a programmed month to month move of $100, or open a financial records and connect it to your venture account.

Set up your record with the broker based on your personal preference. Setting up a venture account isn't very different than setting up any sort of ledger. The entire procedure shouldn't take you more than a couple of moments to finish online.

- Link your financial balance and make your underlying store or move of assets. It might take a couple of days for the cash to be accessible for you to use to purchase stocks.

While you're pausing, you can keep on finding out about the stock market and investing systems.

- You may likewise need to set up a programmed week by week or month to month move from your ledger to your speculation account. If your salary changes, you can likewise make your very own commitments when it's doable to do so.

Research stocks widely before you purchase. Online brokers have data accessible legitimately on the stage for stocks you can purchase.

They may likewise have instructional assets on how to pick the best stocks. In any case, if you don't have a great deal of cash, look past your broker's foundation as well.

- Check the organization's history and the stock's presentation in the course of the last 5 or 10 years.

Decide if there have been any significant changes at the official level as of late, or if the organization has any new items turning out. These are things that could affect the stock cost.

- Full-administration brokers would have the option to offer you loads of guidance on which stocks to pick and how to fabricate your portfolio.

However, if you don't have a great deal of cash to contribute, a full-administration broker is likely not possible. This implies you'll have to do most of the exploration yourself.

Tip: You can investigate a stock outline and friends news on the organization's site. Likewise, search for investigation and articles on money related sites and in monetary productions, like the Wall Street Journal.

Pick 1 or 2 stocks you need to purchase. You may have heard that portfolios ought to be differentiated.

However, if you just have a limited quantity of cash, it's smarter to place the entirety of that cash into 1 or 2 organizations. Pick organizations that have a past filled with strength and profitability.

- If you've limited your enthusiasm to a handful of stocks, pick 1 or 2 that are as of now in a downtrend. After an rise in price, even the most steady and gainful stocks will in general chill for a piece.

If you purchase, then, you stand the best possibility of gaining a decent benefit on the stock.

Increment your property as your record balance develops. Develop the money balance in your speculation account, then do another round of investing. Similarly, as in the past, put resources into 1 or 2 organizations.

Attempt to pick organizations that aren't in a similar industry as the principal organizations you chose.

- By investing limited quantities bit by bit, you'll, in the long run, have a profound, well-broadened portfolio.

- Once you have 5 or 6 unique stocks, allocate your commitment among the stocks to keep your portfolio adjusted. For instance, if a stock is over-performing and has a significant expense, you would ordinarily buy less of that stock.

See whether your boss has a 401(k) plan. While you likely got data about your manager's retirement plan during the direction, that data may have become mixed up in the mix as you changed in accordance with your new position.

Also, most managers expect you to work with them for in any event 60 or 90 days before you become qualified to take an interest in any retirement plan.

- You can check through your direction materials or representative handbook in the event that you have one. If not, ask your chief or somebody in HR. They ought to have the option to give you more data.

Pick a customary 401(k) or a Roth 401(k). Numerous businesses offer two kinds of retirement plans.

The principal contrast between the two is whether you pay now or later. Commitments to a conventional 401(k) are taken from pre-charge dollars, while Roth commitments are taken from your salary after duties.

- Someone in HR will have the option to stroll through the options accessible. However, they won't have the option to offer you any individual venture guidance.

Assess your investment options. You'll likely be placed in contact with an arrangement manager who will select you in the arrangement and kick you off with dealing with your ventures.

Generally, 401(k) directors offer diverse common assets, including list reserves.

Your plan overseer will give you data about the sorts of investments accessible. You might need to do additional research or speak to a monetary counselor if you don't think you realize enough to settle on the best choice.

Contribute a little part of your wages or compensation. At the point when you're simply beginning, you likely don't have a great deal of squirm room in your spending limit. However, you can ordinarily handle contributing 1 or 2 percent of your check to your 401(k).

- If you are paid a time-based compensation, your boss may likewise enable you to contribute a particular dollar sum out of every check to your 401(k), rather than a rate. Once in a while, this can be as low as $1 to $5 per check.

- Check your manager's match when choosing how much of your salary to contribute. Businesses may coordinate 50 to 100 percent of your commitments, up to a most extreme level of your compensation (commonly somewhere in the range of 3 to 6 percent).

Since the boss match is free cash, you need to get as much of this as you can.

Think before you jump! Business coordinating assets might be dependent upon a vesting period. If you leave the organization before that period closes, you won't get any of that cash. You'll generally get the chance to keep your commitments, however.

Increase your commitment when you get a salary increase. Each time you get an increase in salary, disperse half of that add up to compensation and the other half to your 401(k) commitments. That way your investments are expanding yet, you won't miss the cash.

For a model, assume you were contributing 2 percent of your compensation to your 401(k), and you just got a 2 percent increase in salary.

You could build your investment to 3 percent. If your manager coordinates to 6 percent, you've maximized your boss' coordinating.

You don't need to be wealthy to figure out how to put resources into stocks.

Just 55% of Americans put resources into the stock market in 2019. That is down from 63% of Americans who have put resources into stocks legitimately (through values), or by implication (ETFs, shared assets or retirement investment accounts) in 2004.

Of the individuals who contribute, a few people enroll the assistance of a money related guide who makes a ton of the fundamental investment choices for them.

Be that as it may, not every person has the opportunity, cash and confidence expected to utilize a money related consultant.

The uplifting news? Investing in the stock market does have a lower boundary to passage than at any time in recent memory.

Here's a concise breakdown of how to put resources into stocks for beginners. Ensure you're prepared and ready to contribute.

Similarly, as one strolls before they run, so too does one spare before they contribute. That appears glaringly evident, yet this probably won't be:

The general guideline is to have in any event a half year of everyday costs set aside should fiasco strike before you can begin purchasing stocks.

What's more, all charge card obligation ought to be paid off before you set off to become Gordon Gekko 2.0.

The interest you pay on charge card is regularly 15% to 25%.

Paying that down is the least demanding approach to promise yourself an arrival that high on your cash, with free trading applications like Robin Hood.

CHARACTERIZE OBJECTIVES
Putting something aside for a vehicle? House? School? Retirement? Would you like to make easy money, or would you say you are out to win market returns on whatever additional cash you can?

These are altogether different targets, and sincerely characterizing your objective is the initial step to fruitful stock market investing – for beginners and veterans the same.

If you know precisely how much cash you need and when, you can figure what you'll have to normally contribute, accepting a certain rate of return.

Financial specialists ought to have sensible objectives and ensure they are additionally utilizing practical paces of profits on their projections.

"Utilizing a 12% pace of return is altogether different than utilizing a 7% or 8% pace of return," says Ryan Marshall, guaranteed money related organizer and employee of Ela Financial Group.

Shopping center to begin with – albeit beginning with $1,000 to $2,000 makes things a lot simpler.

You don't need enormous sums when first beginning. With only a couple of pennies for every buy, you'll be en route to making savings. As you can envision, this can begin appreciating rapidly.

It's a simple and easy approach to begin investing with next to no cash. With $500 you should utilize a discount broker to execute your trades — full help brokers and their higher bonus charges won't bode well.

There are numerous options with regards to limit brokers. However, your moderate beginning investment will constrain your options, the same number of requiring higher sums just to open a record.

Small issues are not a problem as long as you have acclimated yourself with the risks and rewards. How about we start by considering the measure of risk capital you will require to play the trading or investing game.

The base offset with which you can open a record with even the most profound rebate brokers is $500. Along these lines, in fact, you can't start trading with just a "hundred bucks." That isn't to say that individuals don't begin trading with just $500.

Most online brokers publicize that you can start trading with as little as that. Honestly, there is no trick; they won't punish you for having a little record.

Anyways, when you start trading with a modest amount of money, you constrain yourself since you limit your chances for progress.

For instance, consider if you make a trade and lose $200 of your $500, you have additionally restricted how much cash you have accessible for your next business.

In the condition, if you lose another $200 then you should stop since your odds of success are thin. The straightforward certainty is that you need enough cash to take into consideration various progressive misfortunes in your trading.

You are obviously better off holding up a year to aggregate a decent beginning measure of capital than you are at the beginning with just two or three hundred dollars.

The less you start with, the less your chances of progress. If you should start investing in stocks at $500, there are a couple of approaches to improve your odds of achievement.

The ideal route is to place your cash into common assets. What we're saying is that if you just have $500, you should place it into a modest investment that will be handled by proficient traders in a huge pool of cash.

Expertly overseen common assets can be purchased and sold along these lines to stocks. At the point when you purchase a shared reserve, you are basically giving your cash to the store supervisor who puts it in various stocks the person in question accepts will be productive.

The advantages include a presentation to a more extensive number of stocks just as the entrance to the judiciousness and aptitude of an expert speculator.

Albeit shared assets can be traded somewhat, we don't propose you attempt to do this. Such assets are intended for long haul investment, and the genuine prizes of investing in common assets are regularly observed merely following quite a while to 10 years.

If you need to begin investing somewhat more proactively, set aside your money until you have more than $500. All things considered, $1000 would be a vastly improved beginning sum. Truth be told, we would recommend this as the absolute minimum sum.

If you start investing with $500, it's critical to consider it a strong beginning stage. When you open a record and start investing, your best course of action ought to be to develop your investment stake.

You should plan to add $50 to $100 every month; through finance commitments you can coordinate store cash into numerous investment records or some other ordinary commitment strategy.

If your underlying investment is $500, and you include $100 every month, toward the year's end you will have $1,700 in contributed reserves — in addition to investment pay earned.

As your investment finance develops, so will your investment options. You will, in the long run, have the option to put resources into assets with higher starting investment essentials, just like individual stocks.

And if you intend to be a functioning trader sooner or later, having a more prominent measure of capital to contribute will be significant.

In any case, meanwhile, never permit the way that you have "just" two or three hundred dollars shield you from investing in the stock market.